not
mere
words

not mere words

IGNITING A PASSION
FOR SCRIPTURE

Ryan Dalgliesh

TATE PUBLISHING
AND ENTERPRISES, LLC

Published by Tate Publishing & Enterprises, LLC
127 E. Trade Center Terrace | Mustang, Oklahoma 73064 USA
1.888.361.9473 | www.tatepublishing.com

Tate Publishing is committed to excellence in the publishing industry. The company reflects the philosophy established by the founders, based on Psalm 68:11,
"The Lord gave the word and great was the company of those who published it."

Book design copyright © 2012 by Tate Publishing, LLC. All rights reserved.
Cover and Interior design by Lucia Kroeger Renz

Published in the United States of America

ISBN: 978-1-62024-574-3
1. Religion / Christian Life / Personal Growth
2. Religion / Christian Life / Spiritual Growth
12.06.07

dedication

I want to dedicate this book to my son, Ryker Noble Dalgliesh. I long for you to grow up and become a student of God's Word. It is through the Scripture that you will find direction power for living. God will make himself known through it. It will shape you into a man who has a deep love for the Savior.

I love you.

acknowledgements

I would like to thank the people who helped make this project come together so quickly. Michele, you are a sweet and gracious bride to let me just live at the library for a week to hammer this out. Thanks for your constant encouragement in all that I pursue. I couldn't do these things without you. Kevin and Lakan, thanks for making me throw away the first draft and start all over. I know it was worth the time. Thanks to Laura who was a quick and diligent reader. I really appreciate you checking all of the Scripture references. That was a big task. Thanks to Jason for your suggestions (even though it required me writing another section when I thought I was finished). Thanks to Lance for help with the title. Amanda, this book is going to be my best one yet, and it is all because of the time you spent editing it for me. You have been a tremendous help.

Thanks to all of the people who continue to love, adore, and preach the Bible. You press me further into the heart of God.

Thanks.

table of contents

introduction

Read your Bible and love it, for in it you find your life!

That is it! That is the whole point of this little book you hold in your hands. I want you to love the word of God. I want you to find yourself compelled to proclaim the worth of Jesus in your worship. I want to see you have victory over sin in your life. I deeply long to see families rise up with a passion for knowing God and making him known. I ache to see men who will faithfully teach the truth of the beautiful gospel message of Jesus Christ. I want you to know more about Jesus each day for the rest of your life. All of these things come through a disciplined study and adoration of the word of God.

There are 31,173 verses in the Bible. (Some people disagree on what verses should be included.) That means that you would have to know 311 verses to know one percent of the Bible. The Book of Philippians has 104 verses. In other words, if you know a book the size of Philippians, you know one third of one percent of the Bible. Some people are not good with percents, so look at it this way: knowing the full

Bible would be like having one million dollars. If you knew ten percent, or about 3,117 verses, that would be like having $100,000 in your pocket. If you knew one percent, or 312 verses, that would be like having $10,000 in your pocket. If you knew a book the size of Philippians, that would be equivalent to having $3,336.32 in your pocket. If you only know around ten verses, like most churchgoers, then that would be the equivalent of having $320.80 in your pocket.

Or think about it like this: for every verse you know, you get to put just $32.08 in your pocket. No wonder our lives are in such spiritual poverty. No wonder Christians feel overrun by their circumstances. No wonder we feel so powerless.

We walk around wondering why our marriages are not better, why we keep struggling with the same sin, and why we cannot overcome depression or anger. We wonder why we lack compassion, why it is that we find God boring, or why we struggle with basic truths of the faith. The answer is almost always the same: we do not read or know the Holy Scriptures. We have a wealth of treasures available to us in the Bible, and we are content to get our token thirty minutes a week from the preacher—never even realizing or comprehending that we are going spiritually bankrupt.

To put it another way, what if you were facing surgery tomorrow, and just before you went under the knife, the surgeon said, "Don't worry. I know just less than one percent of this procedure. But I'm sure I'll just figure it out as I go along"? Would you stay there? Would you risk the surgery? No way! That doctor does not know what he is doing. What about a mechanic who knew less than one percent of how to fix a car or a contractor who knew less than one percent about building a house? Would you trust them with your car or your home? Would you sit under a math teacher who did not know math or an art teacher who only knew physics?

Have you felt hopeless yet? Have you felt like you are not gaining ground with Christ? Is your spiritual life stagnant and at a standstill? The next question then has to be, "Are you reading and learning Scripture?" Christians, let us not be uneducated in Scripture. There are a thousand things that you can get by in this life without knowing, but Scripture is not one of them. We ought not to be ignorant people. Let us be learned and educated in many things, but let us first be educated in the Holy Scriptures that gave us life through Jesus Christ!

The truth is that most of us as Christians are trying to do the right thing. We go to church, sing the songs, drop the tithe check into the offering plate, and even pray when a need arises. Sometimes we give a little extra to the missionary who comes to the church every fall. We have been greeters and Sunday school leaders and even helped with Vacation Bible School, donating not only supplies but our time, as well. At work, we have a cross hanging in our cubicle, and we have the little fish stuck to the back of our bumpers. Nevertheless, something is missing. We can feel it. We hear the stories of the people who seem to experience God more richly and more intimately than we do. We wonder why our hearts do not break for the wounded, why we do not shed tears for the lost, and why we sometimes feel like God is so distant that our prayers have not made it to his feet in years.

Sometimes when we are alone, the words "God, where are you?" play across our brains, though we would never let them be heard from our lips. We hear of people who with great force have seen sin patterns broken in their lives by God's grace, and we sit there wondering what we have done wrong that the same sin has stalked us daily for ten or twenty years. We lie in bed at night, tormented by that sin we shamefully harbor. Somewhere along the way, we gave up and resigned ourselves to the idea of having to live with this secret enemy. We men look at our families, and though we love them deeply, we know that we have not led them, have not prayed with them, and have not taught them as we should. Our kids struggle with who God really is, and we throw another cliché at them, knowing that somehow it is not really helping. The basic truths we thought we learned of God as children seemed to carry us quite contentedly for a while. But now with the loss of a job, the bad report from the doctor, the endless calls from collectors, the marriage counseling that seems to be failing, and the ever mounting pressure to "be something more," we hang our heads wondering where it all went so wrong. Let me see if I can explain it.

When we met Jesus at the cross, when we came to the place where we recognized our sinfulness, and when we pleaded with the merciful God to save us through the blood of his Son, something changed in us. "If anyone is in Christ, *he is* a new creation. The old *has passed away*; behold, the new has come" (2 Corinthians 5:17—emphasis mine). You have received the Holy Spirit of God alive in you and have stepped away from the person of sinful flesh that you used to be. "You are not in the flesh but in the Spirit, if in fact the Spirit of God dwells in you. Anyone who does not have the Spirit of Christ does not belong to him" (Romans 8:9). "Do not lie to one another, seeing that you have put off the old self with its practices and have put on the new self, which is being renewed in knowledge after the image of its creator" (Colossians 3:9, 10). Maybe your new self is not being "renewed."

Do you feel that way sometimes? Stagnant? Stuck? Maybe even going backward? You cannot be renewed without knowledge; you cannot teach or be taught apart from the Word of God. You cannot even sing songs of praise and worship to God apart from the truth that is revealed to us in the Holy Scripture. "Let the word of Christ *dwell in you richly,* teaching and admonishing one another in all wisdom, singing psalms and hymns and spiritual songs, with thankfulness in your hearts to God" (Colossians

3:16—emphasis mine). Is God's Word dwelling in you richly? *Richly?* Does the word come alive for you as you read it, or have you limited your daily intake to the 250-word devotional on your nightstand that has one verse on the top of the page? Can one verse a day sustain you? "Man shall not live by bread alone, but by every word that comes from the mouth of God" (Matthew 4:4, Deuteronomy 8:3). We must love the Word.

To be readers and not *lovers* of the Bible will leave us with pillars of plaster for our faith that will crumble at the first sign of affliction. Lovers of God's Word will be changed by it, strengthened against the onslaught of the mightiest gale, and refreshed by the coolness of it in their hearts and minds like water to a thirsty tree. The Word of God will produce in us life, and the fruit of it will be evident in every season that we may walk upon this earth. "But be doers of the word, and not hearers only, deceiving yourselves" (James 1:22).

> Everyone who hears these words of mine and does them will be like a wise man who built his house on the rock. And the rain fell, and the floods came, and the winds blew and beat on that house, but it did not fall, because it had been founded on the rock. And everyone who hears these words of mine and does not do them will be like a foolish man who built his house on the sand. And the rain fell,

and the floods came, and the winds blew and beat against that house, and it fell, and great was the fall of it.

Matthew 7:24-27

Blessed is the man who walks not in the counsel of the wicked, nor stands in the way of sinner, nor sits in the seat of scoffers; but his delight is in the law of the LORD, and on his law he meditates day and night. He is like a tree planted by streams of water that yields its fruit in its season, and its leaf does not wither. In all that he does, he prospers.

Psalm 1:1-3

It is time for us to mature. We came to Christ for salvation, and like newborn babies we began this journey with Christ. We were "born again, not of perishable seed but of imperishable, through the living and abiding word of God; for 'All flesh is like grass and all its glory like the flower of grass. The grass withers, and the flower falls, but the word of the Lord remains forever.' And this word is the good news that was preached to you" (1 Peter 1:23-25). It was God's holy Word that brought to us the beautiful knowledge of salvation through Jesus Christ, and it is by the word that we will mature. "Like newborn infants, long for the pure spiritual milk [of the word], that by it you may grow up to salvation—if indeed you have tasted that the Lord is good" (1 Peter 2:2, 3). Let us not remain as spiritual children but let us grow up to maturity. May it no longer be said of us that we "need milk, not solid food, for everyone who lives on milk is unskilled in the word of righteousness, since he is a child" (Hebrews 5:11-14). Rather, let us move on to the solid food that is for those who are mature and who have trained themselves in the things of righteousness. No more excuses. No more shall we declare that we are too busy or that reading the Bible is for the preacher. No more will we put it off until tomorrow.

If you will journey with me through these few pages, I will show you how the word of God can impact your Christian life, your family, your knowledge of Jesus, and your worship.

God is not done with you! He has a wealth of things to show you, a banquet of truth for you to feed on—and the wealth of his Word is greater than finest gold, and his banquet tastier than the sweetest honey (Psalm 19:10).

Become rich in him!

"Taste and see that the LORD is good!" (Psalm 34:8).

the necessity
of Scripture in
the Christian life

To be honest, this chapter could be a four hundred-page book all by itself, but my attempt in this project is to write something that you can read through easily and quickly. That being said, I am going to try to narrow our field of view for this particular chapter down to three main points: the Bible (via the Holy Spirit) guards us from sin, teaches us about holiness, and turns our eyes to the return of Jesus. However, we must first begin with several understandings between us.

- God's intent was that we be made in and reflect his image (Genesis 1:26, 27).

- Adam's sin broke the image of God and now we are all born in the image of sinful man (Romans 5:12, Romans 3:23).

- The sin that lives in us deserves the full wrath of God and death (Romans 6:23, John 3:36, Romans 2:5).

- Jesus, the full representation of God's glory and the fullness of his power and deity, came as a man and lived a perfect life, was crucified on a cross shedding his blood for the redemption of man, and was resurrected from the dead, restoring our relationship with God by bearing our sin and giving us his righteousness, thereby rescuing us from the wrath of God (John 1:1-14, Hebrews 1:3, Colossians 1:15-20, Colossians 2:9, 1 Corinthians 15:1-4, Ephesians 1:7, 1 Corinthians 1:30, 2 Corinthians 5:21, Romans 5:6-10).

- Our faith in Jesus Christ as Lord and God brings us salvation. We are powerless on our own to save ourselves and can only be saved through Jesus (Acts 4:12, Romans 10:9-10, 13, Ephesians 2:8-10).

- Subsequently, the image of God that was broken in us through sin has been replaced through the work of Jesus. We are now in the process of being conformed to the likeness of Jesus more and more as we journey in this life through the process of sanctification, which is the displined removal of our old sinful self and the daily adherence to the things of God. This process will be completed upon the return of Jesus Christ and the glorification of our bodies (Romans 8:29, Colossians 3:9-10, Ephesians 4:22-24, 1 John 3:1-2).

- We have now been given the Holy Spirit of God as a seal and guarantee of our salvation in Jesus Christ, and he will guide us into all truth and teach us the things of Jesus (Ephesians 1:13, Ephesians 4:30, John 16:13, 1 John 2:27).

GUARDED FROM SIN

"You who love the LORD, hate evil" (Psalm 97:10). We want to, do we not? We want to kill the sin that lives in us and see it removed from our hearts. We long to end the war that wages in our souls as the pugilists named Spirit and Flesh battle for control of our moments (Galatians 5:16-23). We find that the sins we do not want to do we continue doing and the holiness we long to exhibit continues to escape us (Romans 7:15-25). We know that Jesus has set us free from slavery to sin; we are no longer of the flesh (Romans 6:15-18). And yet we find daily that our paths are strewn with deadfalls and mines meant to maim and destroy us. So we press forward, ashamed of our sinful wounds and oozing sores that mark every moment of failure and every instant of defeat. We face each new day looking less like the new creatures that God has made us to be and more like zombies. We have become the living dead, animated and moving onward, but riddled with decay and groaning in sorrow for another lost battle to sin, another wound, another scar.

But this is not the life we were saved to live! The hero has rescued us from this villain. Sin has already been defeated. The reason we so often feel hopeless lies not in the fact that we are somehow still destined for failure but rather that we have not been equipping ourselves with the tools necessary to experience a life that is guarded from sin.

We can keep our ways pure by guarding ourselves according to God's word. The Word of God will guard us and protect us as we store it up in our hearts (Psalm 119:9, 11). We can be confident that sin, a villainous enemy, will relentlessly pursue us and seek to see us destroyed. Sin will not come to us with fangs bared and claws clicking the pavement. Rather, it will come to us with flattering and oily words designed to gain our trust. Yet we can be guarded from it. We can be aware of sin's ploys.

The first nine chapters of the book of Proverbs talk about two women. There is a woman, Adultery, who represents everything that is sinful and set against God. There is also a woman, Wisdom; she represents all that is holy and righteous. Proverbs 9 tells us that both of these women have made their houses on the heights of the city, and both women are offering a meal to the passersby. Both women call out to the "simple" and those "who lacks sense." The promise of Wisdom is that her meal will give us life and insight, but Adultery beckons us to a meal that will lead us to death (Proverbs 9:1-6, 13-18). How can we discern one voice from the other? How can we know which meal gives life and which meal kills? The answer again is the Scripture. When we have left infancy in the things of God and have moved on from the basics of God's Word to those issues that mature us and grow us, we will find that our "powers of discernment [have been] trained by constant practice to distinguish good from evil" (Hebrews 5:11-14). But how can we expect to easily and readily recognize the difference between that which may kill us and that which gives us life if we do not know what the Bible teaches?

I have an uncle who is a physical therapist. Every time I hurt myself or have an ache, I give him a call. Recently, I really hurt my shoulder. I could not pick up my son, carry a bag of ice, sleep on my side at night, or raise my arm above my head. For weeks, I was in pain. I got online and self-diagnosed. (I know, I know, but you do it, too.) I was certain that I had separated the AC joint in my shoulder. The next day, I spoke to my uncle and described to him what was going on over the phone. Without seeing my injury, he told me what he expected it to be (inflammation in the joint) and what the treatment would be (a cortisone shot and some rest). When I saw the doctor the following week, he told me that I had inflammation in the joint and that

I would need a shot and some rest. Before long, I was as good as new.

Here is my point. Why was my uncle able to identify my problem sight unseen, and why was I so convinced it was something else? Simple—years of practice and years of treating injuries has trained my uncle to discern one type of pain from another. I, on the other hand, am a preacher, an artist, and a fisherman. Unfortunately, none of my skills equip me to identify the sources of pain in my body. My uncle did not get to that point overnight. He went to school, studied, graduated, opened a practice, and treated patients for twenty-nine years. He has been trained to discern various pains and the treatments for them. The same is true of our spiritual lives. How can we expect to identify the voice in our heads or in our hearts as belonging to Wisdom or Adultery if we have not been trained by God by his disciplining us through his word into mature adults?

We servants of God are warned by his word and find that in keeping it there is great reward (Psalm 19:11).

Consider this text from Proverbs 2:

> My son, if you *receive* my words and *treasure* up my commandmentswithin you, making your ear *attentive to wisdom* and inclining your heart to *understanding*; yes, if you *call out for insight* and raise your voice *for understanding*, if you *seek it* like silver and search for it as for hidden treasures, then you will understand the fear of the LORD and find

the knowledge of God. For the LORD gives wisdom; from his mouth come knowledge and understanding; he stores up sound wisdom for the upright; *he is a shield* to those who walk in integrity, *guarding* the paths of justice and *watching over the way of his saints.*

Then you will understand righteousness and justice and equity, every good path; for *wisdom will come into your heart* and *knowledge will be pleasant to your soul; discretion will watch over you, understanding will guard you, delivering you from the way of evil,* from men of perverted speech, who forsake the paths of uprightness to walk in the ways of darkness, who rejoice in doing evil and delight in the perverseness of evil, men whose paths are crooked, and who are devious in their ways. So *you will be delivered* from the forbidden woman, from the adulteress with her smooth words, who forsakes the companion of her youth and forgets the covenant of her God; for her house sinks down to death, and her paths to the departed, none who go to her come back, nor do they regain the paths of life. So you will walk in the way of the good and keep to the paths of the righteous. For the upright will inhabit the land, and those with integrity will remain in it, but the wicked will be cut of from the land, and the treacherous will be rooted out of it (emphasis mine).

Receive God's Word. Treasure up all of his commandments. Listen to wisdom. Turn your heart to understanding. Call out to God for insight and raise your voice to the heavens to understand the person of our Great God. Seek for wisdom like you would silver—in the same way you would pursue a buried treasure. Then you *will* understand what it means to fear the LORD, and you will gain knowledge of the Holy One. God will be a shield to you and guard all of your steps, watching over all of your ways. Righteousness, justice, equity, and every good path will dwell in your heart through wisdom. The knowledge of God will be pleasant and refreshing to your soul. Your bodyguards will be discretion and understanding, and they will safely deliver you from the sinful ways that plague you like a disease. When you embrace wisdom, you will find yourself delivered from the smooth-talking, villainous, adulterous woman who seeks to kill you. You will gain treasures of life through your pursuit of the wisdom of God as you mine it like jewels from the mountain of the Scripture.

One final thought on this section: Proverbs 5, speaking of the traitorous woman Adultery, says her "lips drip honey, her speech is smoother than oil, but in the end she is bitter as wormwood, *sharp as a two-edged sword*" (Proverbs 5:3, 4—emphasis mine).

We all know that sin can cut. We can look back on times in our lives when someone else's sin has left wounds and scars in us. We can remember times when our own sin came close to destroying us. We reflect on the severity of it, and we agree with this verse that sin is indeed as "sharp as a two-edged sword."

However, there is another verse nestled in the Scripture that gives us hope. It gives us more than hope in fact. This other verse gives us cause to say, "Aha! I have you now, you vile dragon. No more shall I be taken in by your slippery words." When we turn to Hebrews 4:12, we find our answer and our source of power and victory. "For the Word of God is living and active, *sharper than any two-edged sword*" (emphasis mine). Look at the significance of that phrase. Sin is *as sharp as a two-edged sword*, but the Word of God is *sharper than any two-edged sword*.

Sin is sharp. God's Word is sharper!

Sin can cut us and wound us. God's Word can defeat that which cuts and wounds!

Sin can pierce us. God's Word can shatter sin!

Oh, Christian, seek after wisdom that you may be guarded from sin but also that you may embrace the righteousness of God.

EMBRACING HOLINESS

If you are a Christian, then God has already made you righteous (2 Corinthians 5:21, Philippians 3:8, 9). You have put on the righteousness of Christ and have already been made completely holy.

So many Christians misunderstand holiness. We do not become more holy. Holiness is not a matter of what we can do or what we cannot do. Holiness is only found in the person of Jesus. Think about it like this: as a believer, you are already a child of God. You are not sort of a child of God. You are completely adopted into the family of Christ, and you now have boldness to call God your Father (Romans 8:15, Galatians 4:5, 6). You are completely forgiven. You are not partially forgiven or only forgiven on Thursdays. You are totally and irreversibly forgiven by Jesus. The issue is not getting more forgiveness or more adoption or more holiness. Because of the finished work of Christ Jesus on the cross, you are completely forgiven, fully integrated into the family of God, and completely holy in the sight of your heavenly Father. So then, as I said, we are not trying to become more holy. Rather, since we have been made holy by God, we are commanded to behave as holy people.

Think of the difference in those two words *become* and *behave*. You have already *become* holy, so now our duty is to *behave* that way. You are already a child of God, so act like you are. You have already been completely forgiven, so quit living like a rebel. We have been changed, so we should behave like we have been changed. Do not be conformed to the pattern of this world, seek the things of this earth, or live in your former sins. Put off your old ways, the old patterns of life, and change how you think. Focus on the things of heaven, look to God, and follow his example of holiness. Just because we are wholly forgiven, wholly adopted, and wholly holy does not mean we know right away how to behave properly.

That is where the Bible comes in. It trains us. "All Scripture is breathed out by God and profitable for teaching, for reproof, for correction, and for training in righteousness, that the man of God may be competent, equipped for every good work" (2 Timothy 3:16-17). The Bible shows us how to behave as new people. We should not be embarrassed that we do not know how to behave as Christians, but we also should not be happy to stay ignorant. We should want to know what it looks like to love God more deeply. After all, we demonstrate that we truly love our great and glorious God through our obedience to his commands. The only way we know what God requires of us is to know the Word.

The works of the flesh in us are obvious, but we are systematically putting them to death through reliance on the Spirit and the study of the Word. The question then becomes, "What do we replace them with?" The answer comes in Galatians. "The fruit of the Spirit is love, joy, peace, patience, kindness, goodness, faithfulness, gentleness, self-control; against such things there is no law" (Galatians 5:22, 23). When we have put off sexual immorality, impurity, passions, evil desires, covetousness, anger, wrath, malice, slander, and obscene talk from our mouths with an understanding of Scripture, by the grace of God, through the blood of Jesus, and in the instruction of the Holy Spirit, we find that it is only right that those things be replaced. We put on, then, as God's chosen ones who are holy and beloved by him, compassion, kindness, humility, meekness, patience, forgiveness, love, and peace. We do this through the rich indwelling of God's Word in our hearts (Colossians 3:1-16).

When we have come to the place where we wish to see ourselves no longer conformed to the world and no longer conformed to the sinful patterns that were ours in our former ignorance, but rather to be holy in all of our behavior as God is holy, we find that we *must* cling to the word of God, having our minds soberly set upon being renewed through it (Romans 12:1-2, 1 Peter 1:13-16). We daily pursue putting off the old self and putting on the new self. We are made more and more into the image of Christ with each passing moment.

If it is true that Paul did not know what covetousness was apart from the Law (Romans 7:7), then how can a person know what righteousness is apart from the Word? We have a list of things we are to be about as followers of Christ. How can we know what love looks like without the Bible? What about joy, peace, holiness, forgiveness, meekness, humility, compassion, self-control, gentleness, faithfulness, goodness, kindness, and patience? These things are found in Christ alone, and if we do not know what the Bible teaches about Jesus, then we have settled for a worldly, fleshly view of the One who should be known only in the fullness of his glory and power. If we do not know God's person and nature, we cannot know love (1 John 4:8). We cannot stumble into more patience. We do not accidentally become more compassionate. Self-control does not fall out of the sky and land at our feet. These are the things we come by through the diligent and disciplined study of the Word.

Is your life marked by these things?

> Make every effort to supplement your faith with virtue, and virtue with knowledge, and knowledge with self-control, and self-control with steadfastness, and steadfastness with godliness, and godliness with brotherly affection, and brotherly affection with love. For if these qualities are yours *and are increasing*, they keep you from being ineffective or unfruitful in the knowledge of our Lord Jesus Christ. For whoever lacks these qualities is so nearsighted that he is blind, having forgotten that he was cleansed from his former sins. Therefore, brothers, be all the more diligent to make your calling and

election sure, for if you practice these qualities *you will never fall.*

2 Peter 1:5-10 (emphasis mine)

If these things are lacking in your life, it begs the question, "Are you daily in the Scripture and in love with it?"

Do not think of the Word only as a simple line in the sand, dividing right from wrong; remember that the Word of God teaches us to set our eyes on the coming of our great Savior Jesus.

LOOKING FOR JESUS

The simple truth is that the Christian is all too often concerned with the ins and outs of each little day on this earth. We would do better to have our eyes fixed firmly on the return of Jesus with all of our hopes and affections hanging on his soon and coming appearance. The Scripture turns our eyes from our own selves and raises them heavenward. No more do we look only to tomorrow, but rather we set our eyes on that great and glorious last day! God's Word makes the future realization of Christ's coming leap to the forefront of our thoughts, dispelling the shadows of this dreary life that besets us. If only we could be like Job and see past the destruction of our earthly bodies to that glorious day when we will behold our Redeemer with our very own eyes.

> I know that my Redeemer lives, and at the last he
> will stand upon the earth. After my skin has been
> thus destroyed, yet in my flesh I shall see God, whom
> I shall see for myself, and my eyes shall behold, and
> not another. [Oh how] my heart faints within me!

> Job 19: 25-27

I confess that for many years my heart did not faint with longing for the return of Christ. But now, "I believe that I shall look upon the goodness of the LORD in the land of the living!" (Psalm 27:13). "I shall behold [his] face in righteousness; when I awake, I shall be satisfied with [his] likeness" (Psalm 17:15). I know that this present heavens and earth shall pass away with a roar, and I shall wait for and hasten the coming of the day of God (2 Peter 3:7-14). All of my hope is fully set on the grace that will be brought to me when Christ Jesus is revealed (1 Peter 1:13). "In a moment, in the twinkling of an eye the trumpet shall sound, and the dead will be raised imperishable, and we shall be changed" (1 Corinthians 15:49-57). We will then be conformed into the likeness of Jesus, for we shall see him as he truly is (1 John 3:1-2).

> The Lord himself will descend from heaven with
> a cry of command, with the voice of an archangel,
> and with the sound of the trumpet of God. And the
> dead in Christ will rise first. Then we who are alive,
> who are left, will be caught up together with them

in the clouds to meet the Lord in the air, and *so we will always be with the Lord.*

1 Thessalonians 4:16-17 (emphasis mine)

No more will we weep, hunger shall be abolished, death shall be destroyed, and pain will have ceased. A great multitude beyond counting from all tribes and peoples and languages will stand before the throne of our great redeeming Lamb and will proclaim his worth (Revelation 7: 9-17, Revelation 21:4).

So here I sit as a stranger and an exile on this earth. I am patiently seeking my homeland. I am eagerly longing for my better country—a heavenly one. I am daily groaning for the return of our beautiful Jesus and the glory that will be revealed to me at his return. All of my hope is set on this one fact! (Hebrews 11:13-16, Romans 8:16-25).

The Word of God is necessary for the removal and defeat of sin in our hearts. The Word of God is necessary in producing holiness in us. The Word of God is necessary in turning our eyes to heaven.

Let us be people of the Word!

the necessity
of Scripture
in the family

The family is a painful mystery unless it is understood in terms of the eternal, immortal, invisible King of glory.

I was first a child—a son to my parents. I became a man. I then became a husband to my beautiful bride, Michele. In time, I was blessed to become a father to two wonderful boys, Asher and Ryker. Until I have come hungry for the Scripture and devoured the truth therein, I do not know how to be a child, a man, a husband, or a father. Those are things that I can only realize in a disciplined study of the Word.

It is no mystery what a husband is supposed to look like. It has less to do with earning a paycheck and buying a house than our culture would have you believe. The manner in which a wife should conduct herself is not a riddle. It has less to do with her ability to cook and clean than old sitcoms would imply. What it means to be a child is not a puzzle to be figured out. It is plainly written in Scripture. We, who are in faith, are called the children of God (Romans 8:15-17).

We also know that the Church, all of those who by faith profess the name of Jesus Christ, is called the Bride. Jesus is our glorious bridegroom, and we rejoice "greatly at the bridegroom's voice" (John 3:29). He has clothed us in white and washed us with the water of the word, "so that he might present [us] to himself in splendor, without spot or wrinkle or any such thing, that [we] might be holy and without blemish" Ephesians 5:25-27. He has prepared us for the marriage ceremony and for his wonderful returning. We have prepared ourselves as the Bride by dressing ourselves in righteous deeds that he has prepared beforehand for us to walk in (Revelation 19:7-8, Ephesians 2:10). "Your Maker is your husband, the LORD of hosts is his name; and the Holy One of Israel is your Redeemer, the God of the whole earth he is called" (Isaiah 54:5).

The Scripture is clear that we are the Bride of Christ and he is our husband. We simply wait for him to return for the wedding celebration. We have already been betrothed to him through his fully satisfying work on the cross. We look to Jesus as an example of what it means to be a godly husband.

We know that husbands should "love your wives, as Christ loved the church and gave himself up for her"

(Ephesians 5:25). A good husband will love his bride like Jesus has loved us. How has Jesus loved us? In what manner has he wooed us? His compassions have never ended. His mercy for us is unfathomable. His kindness to us draws us near to him. When we have been unlovely, he has overwhelmed us by his grace. When we have been rebellious, he has been forgiving. When we have been faithless, he has demonstrated his unswerving faithfulness. This is what it looks like to be a husband.

We, as the Bride, have been drawn in to him by his kindness (Romans 2:4). We have respected him. We have loved Jesus our bridegroom by proclaiming his worth. We have submitted ourselves to his trustworthy leadership. This is what it looks like to be a bride.

It is certainly true that it is an easier thing to be the bride of Christ than it is to be the bride to sinful man. It is equally true that it is infinitely difficult to be the kind of husband God has been to us. This is why so many marriages fail and also why we are in daily need of God's present mercy. We husbands must endeavor to serve and love like God has loved us so that we are worthy of being honored by our brides, and wives must remember what it is to respect their heavenly Husband so that they might win over their earthly ones. To know what it is to be the husband and wife we must always view those relationships in light of the love and goodness of God revealed to us through the Scripture.

We, as children, have come under the counsel and tutelage of our Father. He has disciplined us in love so that we would see the peaceful fruit of righteousness borne in our hearts (Hebrews 12:4-11). We do not reject his discipline but we consider it a kindness to us (Psalm 141:5). We do not reject his teachings but submit to them that they may train us. This is what it looks like to be a child.

We who are fathers have seen the kindness of our heavenly Father. We have sat at his feet as children. We have been trained and disciplined, and therefore we know what it means to train and discipline our children in love. We raise them up on the foundation of truth through the living and active Word of God. Our Father has responded more kindly to us than our transgressions against him have deserved, but he has not ignored them. He has loved us through rebellion and loved us through our ignorance so that we might grow into mature men and women. He is pleased with us as children but not pleased to see us remain children. This is what it looks like to be a father.

I know some would look at this and say that God has set too high a standard for the family. I would respond by saying that it is not too high but just high enough. Would we settle for less in our marriages than the example for marriage that Christ set for us? Would we be content for less than the paternal example set for us by God? Would we seek to have our homes fall short of the glory and beauty of Jesus? Let us press on to be perfect even as our heavenly

Father is perfect (Matthew 5:48). Let us desire the perfectly high standard for living in this world, and may we be instructed in the word as we come to hide it in our hearts. Let us learn what the Bible says we are to look like as husband, wife, child, and father.

THE HUSBAND

> Then the LORD God said, "It is not good that the man should be alone; I will make him a helper fit for him." And the rib that the LORD God had taken from the man he made into a woman and brought her to the man. Then the man said, "This at last is bone of my bones and flesh of my flesh; she shall be called Woman, because she was taken out of Man." Therefore a man shall leave his father and his mother and hold fast to his wife, and they shall become one flesh. And the man and his wife were both naked and were not ashamed.
>
> Genesis 2:18-25

We have been joined to our brides. No other relationship carries with it the intimacy that we find between a husband and a bride. We have departed from our parents, and one day our children will depart from us. But as long as we both have the blessing of walking upon this earth, our sweet brides will be one flesh with us. As we will see in Ephesians in a moment, we should love and cherish our brides like we do our very own flesh. We should nourish our brides as we do our own bodies—caring for her and adoring her. Your wife is a blessing from the LORD. Rejoice in her. Be so intoxicated with her that no other woman could ever catch your eye. Stumble over her, fall all over your bride, and be filled with delight by her. "Your wife will be like a fruitful vine within your house... Behold, thus shall the man be blessed who fears the LORD" (Psalm 128:3, 4). "Let your fountain be blessed, and rejoice in the wife of your youth, a lovely deer, a graceful doe. Let her breasts fill you at all times with delight; be intoxicated always in her love" (Proverbs 5:18, 19). "He who finds a wife finds a good thing and obtains favor from the LORD" (Proverbs 18:22). Have you obtained this kind favor from the LORD? You have found a good thing in your wife. You may receive house and wealth from your parents, but a prudent wife comes only from the LORD (Proverbs 19:14).

"Enjoy life with the wife whom you love, all the days of your vain life that he has given you under the sun, because that is your portion in life and in your toil at which you toil under the sun" Ecclesiastes 9:9. Delight in her. Life under the sun is difficult. We toil and toil, but for what? Your portion is not found in your paycheck, and it is not found in your promotion. Roll over in the middle of the night. Reach out your arms. There she is, your portion, your blessing, your favor from God. Enjoy her!

Too often, though, "you cover the Lord's altar with tears, with weeping and groaning because he no longer regards the offering or accepts it with favor from your hand. But you say, 'Why does he not?' Because the Lord was witness between you and the wife of your youth, to whom you have been faithless, though she is your companion and your wife by covenant" (Malachi 2:13-14). Marriage is not simply a matter of a decision we come to casually and that we can depart from just as casually. We have come together under the laws of a covenant between us and God. This is something we should hold to diligently, fearfully, and joyfully. God has made us one, joining us through the Spirit. "And what was the one God seeking? Godly offspring" (Malachi 2:15). You were not joined together only for the epitome of pleasure. You were not bound together by the Spirit in a covenant so that you could get a tax break or only so that you could share your life with someone. You were joined together for the holy purpose of producing godly offspring that the image of God, found in you, would be multiplied in this earth through the children you would have or those who would be your children in the faith.

> So guard yourselves in your spirit, and let none of you be faithless to the wife of your youth. "For the man who hates and divorces, says the Lord, the God of Israel, covers his garment with violence, says the Lord of hosts. So guard yourselves in your spirit, and do not be faithless."
>
> Malachi 2:15-16

Faithlessness to our brides is not only through adultery, but we have been faithless to her when we have been less than the husbands God has called us to be—when we have violated the covenant and when we have failed to nourish her or cherish her. To be faithful to our brides is to be to them what Christ has already modeled to us.

That is why the Scripture reminds us of this:

> Husbands, love your wives, as Christ loved the church and gave himself up for her... In the same way husbands should love their wives as their own bodies. He who loves his wife loves himself. For no one ever hated his own flesh, but nourishes and cherishes it, just as Christ does the church, because we are members of his body. Therefore a man shall leave his father and mother and hold fast to his wife, and the two shall become one flesh. This mystery is profound, and I am saying that it refers to Christ and the church. However, let each one of you love his wife as himself...

> Ephesians 5:25-33

"Husbands, love your wives, and do not be harsh with them" (Colossians 3:19). "Husbands, live with your wives in an understanding way, showing honor to the woman as the weaker vessel, since they are heirs with you of the grace of life, so that your prayers may not be hindered" (1 Peter 3:7). Look to your bride and see one who was redeemed by the blood of Christ in the same way that you were. She, too, is an heir of God and coheir of Jesus. She, too, has the hope of the revelation of the glory of God. Treat her tenderly. God has been a tender husband to us; may we overflow with the tenderness that he has shown us.

THE WIFE

"An excellent wife is the crown of her husband, but she who brings shame is like rottenness to his bones" (Proverbs 12:4). In my book *Love Notes: a Biblical Look at Love,* I talk about how finding a righteous wife is like a treasure hunt. A noble wife is like a crown on the head of a man who was otherwise poor. We men are all simply paupers until we are blessed by God with the woman who would crown us. This is not to say that single men are somehow lesser than married men. Obviously, the single man is able to honor and serve the Lord in great power and lead a rich life. But those of us who have been blessed by God with an excellent bride will attest to the dynamic change she has had in our lives.

Sadly though, many women bring with them rottenness rather than crowning glory. You have the power to bring either glory or shame. But there is no glory other than that which comes from knowing God. If you are to be a crown of glory, then you must be a woman of God—one who drinks in his character and nature and pours it out into your husband, your children, and your home. You can build up your home in strength or tear it down all with your own power. "The wisest of women builds her house, but folly with her own hands tears it down" (Proverbs 14:1). However, you can only build a house by the power of God; otherwise, all of your labor is in vain. (Psalm 127:1). Would you be a woman of glory—a woman who builds up? Then you must be a woman of the Word!

Wives are called to respect their husbands. "Wives, submit to your own husbands, as to the Lord. And let the wife see that she respects her husband" (Ephesians 5:22, 33). "Wives, submit to your husbands, as is fitting in the Lord" (Colossians 3:18). But if you persist in quarreling, you are like a driving rain, and it would be better for your husband if he were to live in the desert or on the corner of the roof than with you (Proverbs 19:13, 21:19, 25:24). "A continual dripping on a rainy day and a quarrelsome wife are alike; to restrain her is to restrain the wind or to grasp oil in one's right hand" (Proverbs 27:15-16).

But if you are submissive to your husbands, even to those who do not obey or love the Word, you may find that "they may be won without a word by the conduct of their wives—when they see your respectful and pure conduct" (1 Peter 3:1-2).

Do not be a woman who is adorned only on the outside.

> But let your adorning be the hidden person of the heart with the imperishable beauty of a gentle and quiet spirit, which in God's sight is very precious.

For this is how the holy women who hoped in God used to adorn themselves, by submitting to their husbands.

1 Peter 3:4-5

Let your adornment be the hidden person of the heart! Wow! That beauty is imperishable because it is the beauty of the imperishable Word of God hidden in your heart (1 Peter 1:23). From your heart flows the springs of life—the Word of God that is hidden therein (Proverbs 4:20-23).

> An excellent wife who can find? She is far more precious than jewels. The heart of her husband trusts in her. She does him good, and not harm, all the days of her life. She works with willing hands. She dresses herself with strength and makes her arms strong. She opens her hand to the poor and reaches out her hands to the needy. Strength and dignity are her clothing, and she laughs at the time to come. She opens her mouth with wisdom, and the teaching of kindness is on her tongue. [But how can wisdom come from a mouth when the heart it is connected to does not know the things of God?] She looks well to the ways of her household and does not eat the bread of idleness. Her children rise up and call her blessed; her husband also, and he praises her: "Many women have done excellently,

but you surpass them all." Charm is deceitful, and beauty is vain, but a woman who fears the LORD is to be praised.

Proverbs 31:10-30

What a wonderful thing to be a wife like this. Your husband would be truly blessed. You are better than any treasure that has ever been unearthed. You are a diligent worker. You long to teach the truth of God. It is okay to be charming and fine to be beautiful, but it is your godly character that will win you true praise.

Fear the Lord, oh women of God. The fear of the Lord is the beginning of all wisdom (Job 28:28, Psalm 111:10, Proverbs 1:7, Proverbs 9:10, Proverbs 15:33, Isaiah 33:5-6, Micah 6:9).

THE CHILDREN

"Behold, children are a heritage from the LORD, the fruit of the womb a reward. Like arrows in the hand of a warrior are the children of one's youth. Blessed is the man who fills his quiver with them!" (Psalm 127: 3-5). "Your children will be like olive shoots around your table. Behold, thus shall the man be blessed who fears the LORD" (Psalm 128:3, 4). If you are under the authority of your parents still, you need to recognize that God has told them that you are a reward and a blessing. Act that way! What does it mean to look like a blessing and a reward? The answer is really quite simple.

Obey them, honor them, and receive their correction. In so doing, you will fill their hearts with joy and bring honor to their names. Ideally, your parents are godly parents who are instructing you in the things of God. But even if they are rebelling against God, the Scripture is clear that your duty is to honor and obey them. This is the right thing to do in the sight of God. Soon enough, you will have departed from your parents' home to make a home for yourself, and God will bless and reward you with children of your own. Your obedience to God now will equip you to train up your children in the things of God when that time comes.

Furthermore, you demonstrate whether you are a wise child or a foolish child by your obedience and your submission to your parents. The discipline they hand down to you is for your own good; do not reject it. Rather, embrace it. If they are godly, then their instruction will guard you from the way of sin and death. Their discipline will shape you for righteous living.

"Hear, O sons, a father's instruction, and be attentive, that you may gain insight" (Proverbs 4:1).

> My son, keep your father's commandment, and forsake not your mother's teaching. Bind them on your heart always; tie them around your neck. When you walk, they will lead you; when you lie down, they will watch over you; and when you awake, they will talk with you. For the commandment is a lamp and the teaching a light, and the reproofs of discipline

are the way of life, to preserve you from the evil woman, from the smooth tongue of the adulteress.

Proverbs 6: 20-24

"A wise son makes a glad father, but a foolish son is a sorrow to his mother" (Proverbs 10:1).

"A wise son hears his father's instruction, but a scoffer does not listen to rebuke" (Proverbs 13:1).

"A wise son makes a glad father, but a foolish man despises his mother" (Proverbs 15:20).

"A foolish son is a grief to his father and bitterness to her who bore him" (Proverbs 17:25).

"The father of the righteous will greatly rejoice; he who fathers a wise son will be glad in him. Let your father and mother be glad; let her who bore you rejoice" (Proverbs 23:24-25).

"Children, obey your parents in the Lord, for this is right. 'Honor your father and mother' (this is the first commandment with a promise), 'that it may go well with you and that you may live long in the land'" (Ephesians 6:1-3).

"Children, obey your parents in everything, for this pleases the Lord" (Colossians 3:20).

Please the Lord by being children who love, honor, and obey your parents.

THE FATHER

Hear, O Israel; The LORD our God, the LORD is one. You shall love the LORD your God with all your heart and with all your soul and with all your might. And these words that I command you today shall be on your heart. You shall teach them diligently to your children, and shall talk of them when you sit in your house, and when you walk by the way, and when you lie down, and when you rise. You shall bind them as a sign on your hand and they shall be as frontlets between your eyes. You shall write them on the doorposts of your house and on your gates.

Deuteronomy 6:4-9

This is such an important text, and Moses is so keen on reminding the parents of this truth that just five chapters later he tells them again.

You shall therefore lay up these words of mine in your heart and in your soul, and you shall bind them as a sign on your hand, and they shall be as frontlets between your eyes. You shall teach them to your children, talking of them when you are sitting in your house, and when you are walking by the way, and when you lie down, and when you rise. You shall write them on the doorposts of your house and on your gates.

Deuteronomy 11:18-20

If you will take the time, you will notice how similar this passage is to Proverbs 6:20-24. In the Proverbs text, the children are encouraged to keep the instruction of their parents. Whether they walk or lie down, they will watch over them. When they are awake, the commandments of their parents will talk with them. The things their parents teach them will guard them from the evil way. Now when we go back to Deuteronomy, we find that we are to be teaching our children the truths of God and his Word. We are to talk about these things whether we are at home or away from home and whether we are lying down with the setting of the sun or rising up to a new day. The Word of God should be so prevalent in our homes that it is written on our hands, bound on our foreheads, buried in our hearts and souls, and written on the doorposts and the gates. Now, I know some people who will post the Scripture over their door in an attempt to obey this text. While there is nothing wrong with this practice, it is futile if the Word is not also in your heart and soul.

Father, when you fail to know the truths of God, you also fail in teaching them to your children. The end result is a house that will crumble and children who will not be guarded from sin. Love your children enough to know the Word of God. Desire God enough to know him and to pour him out in every moment of every day that you lead your family. Let there be no moment when the Word of God is absent from your actions.

"Fathers, do not provoke your children to anger, but bring them up in the discipline and instruction of the Lord" (Ephesians 6:4). Remember that your goal is not to brow beat them nor to humiliate them. Your goal is to bring them up in the same discipline and instruction that the Lord has brought you up in. He does so because of his rich love for you and his desire to see you excel in righteousness. Discipline that comes from anger or frustration is not the discipline of the Lord. Read Hebrews 12:4-11 again to see the purpose of holy discipline. Instruct them in things that bring them life. The Word of God is life (Deuteronomy 32:47). Do not give them your old clichés or trite so-called "manly" advice. Give them the Bible. Human precepts and teachings may indeed appear wise but are of no value in stopping the indulgence of the sinful flesh (Colossians 2:20-23). So, "fathers, do not provoke your children, lest they become discouraged" (Colossians 3:21). Rather, encourage them and spur them on to holiness in all things. Again, let me say that you cannot possibly instruct them in the things of the Lord if you do not know them yourself.

When Paul was writing to the church at Thessalonica, he portrayed his relationship to them at one point like a father to a son. He had fathered them in the faith. But he said something that is interesting, and if we are not careful, we will miss the implication buried there. He says, "For you know how, like a father with his children, we exhorted each one of you and encouraged you and charged you to walk in a manner worthy of God, who calls you into his own kingdom and glory" (1 Thessalonians 2:11, 12). Do you see it? Like a father with his child, we "exhort, encourage, and charge you to walk in a manner worthy of God."

Fathers, please fall so deeply in love with the God of all glory that you can in word and deed "exhort, encourage and charge" your children to walk in a holy life worthy of our God who redeemed us.

Lead from the Bible. Humble yourself before the Spirit and invite him to guide you into all truth so that you can pour that truth into your family.

CLOSING REMARKS

What I said before, I say again; the family is a painful mystery unless it is understood in terms of the eternal, immortal, invisible King of glory. Until we come to the rich truth of Scripture, we will fail as husbands, wives, children, and fathers. Drink in the Bible. Love the word. Let it dwell richly in you! See it raise you and your family up as people who live powerfully in the name of Jesus!

the necessity of Scripture in the practice of worship

The heart of God is not concerned so much with where we worship or when. The heart of God has always been about the object of our worship combined with sincerity and truth. It is neither about worshiping on this mountain or that mountain nor about worshiping at this service or that service. It is about a pure and unadulterated worship of our Holy God. He calls for us to worship him in Spirit and in truth. God is the Everlasting I Am! God is Spirit! God is truth! (John 4:21-24).

Worship that is missing the object of true worship, the Spirit of God or the truth of his personage, is vile and wicked in his sight. Do not assume that simply meeting together and singing songs somehow blesses the heart of God. Let us not be simplistic and shallow in our faith to believe that worship is somehow limited to the fifteen minutes every Sunday morning that we are lifting our voices with other believers. It is possible for your lips to be honoring God as you proclaim truth but to have your heart disconnected from the Spirit. Your lips may be near to God even while your heart is far from him. In that case, your worship is all vanity and worthlessness (Matthew 15:7-9, Isaiah 29:13, Jeremiah 12:2).

Do we really believe that we are true worshipers when we do not even know the character and nature of the God we serve? God hates our solemn assemblies when they are comprised only of lip service. He will not accept your offering of praise and worship when it has been divorced from a love for his character and nature. Our songs are but noise in his ears when we bring worship to him that overlooks his power, glory, and majesty! (Amos 5:21-24, Isaiah 1:10-17). We know the words so well that we can sing them even while planning what we are going to do for lunch—and we call that worship!

When were we last moved by the person of God and his beauty, holiness, righteousness, judgment, mercy, faithfulness, love, compassion, wrath, justice, peace, kindness, and forgiveness? When was the last time that we unfolded the Word of God and gained such understanding that we were compelled to our faces in worship of our Savior (Psalm 119:130)? Does worship even exist for us outside of a predetermined time of the week in a predetermined setting?

Let me say it this way: if worship for us is something we *only* do with a group of people at the start of a service, then we do not yet know what it is to worship. When we fall in love with God—madly deeply in love with him—we are compelled to worship. It cannot be helped. The Bible is so full of examples of worship and is so flooded with instruction on worship that to exhaust them all would take too much time. I have limited myself to some of the Psalms. It is my hope that looking at these passages will make us people who truly worship. My prayer is that God (and not a musical style) will be the object of our worship. My desire is that our worship would be Spirit led and not driven by goose bumps and warm feelings. My earnest longing is that we will proclaim the rich truth of God and not settle for sweet-sounding rhymes. This will be the natural outworking of a disciplined study of the Word. When we read the Word, and let it take root in our hearts, we find that the object of all of our affections is our great God, and we will be moved by the truth that the Spirit has revealed to us.

Oh, that we would worship the Lord in Spirit and truth!

First of all, let our worship be at its very core something that ascribes to God all that is due him and all that he is. To ascribe something to someone is to credit to them something that belongs to them as part of their character—something that flows out of them. We ought to "ascribe to the Lord glory and strength. Ascribe to the Lord the glory due his name; worship the Lord in the splendor of holiness" (Psalm 29:1, 2). What is it that you know of God's glory? What is it that you have heard of his strength?

Have you seen the splendor of his holiness like the sun that breaks through the clouds? Worship him for these things. Declare these things back to him.

> Oh sing to the LORD a new song; sing to the LORD, all the earth! Sing to the LORD, bless his name; tell of his salvation from day to day. Declare his glory among the nations, his marvelous works among all the peoples! For great is the LORD, and greatly to be praised; he is to be feared above all gods. For all the gods of the peoples are worthless idols, but the LORD made the heavens. Splendor and majesty are before him; strength and beauty are in his sanctuary. Ascribe to the LORD, O families of the peoples, ascribe to the LORD glory and strength! Ascribe to the LORD the glory due his name; bring an offering, and come into his courts! Worship the LORD in the splendor of holiness, tremble before him, all the earth!

> Psalm 96:1-9

Let your lips cry out how you have seen his glory displayed on the foothills. Declare with a loud voice how you have seen his glory leap like a roe deer on the mountaintops. Boast of how you have seen God's glory in the fiery sunset that painted the sky in crimson and bathed the earth in golden hues. Tell him how you have been overcome by the revelation of his glory in the thundering waves that crashed upon the cliffs. Speak to him of the strength in his arms that rescue the perishing and redeem those sold into sin. Shout to him with jubilee at the might he displays over all planets, stars, and distant galaxies. Love him for the beauty of holiness that clothes him like a robe and adorns him like a crown. Praise him for his holiness through which we too have been made holy.

Now you have just begun to worship!

> Shout for joy to God … Sing the glory of his name; give to him glorious praise! Say to God, "How awesome are your deeds! *So great is your power that your enemies come cringing to you.* All the earth worships you and sings praises to you; they sing praises to your name. Come and see what God has done: he is awesome in his deeds toward the children of man."
>
> Psalm 66:1-5

There is no god who is like our God. There are no works on this earth that are like the works of our God. *Our God is great and does wonderful things.* He alone is God, and all the nations he has made will come and worship before him (Psalm 86:8-10). What are the wonderful deeds he has done? What are his works in this earth? Remember them, and then worship him for them! He is the God who made heaven and earth. All of creation serves him and owes everything to him. He gives life and breath to all men. He holds all things together by the power of his hand (Acts

17:25, Colossians 1:15-17). He sent his Son to redeem us. While we were powerless, ungodly sinners who were his enemies, he lavished love on us and saved us from the coming wrath (Romans 5:6-10). One day, Jesus will return. And when he does, every knee will bow before him, and all tongues will declare him as Lord, for he will be seen in his full glory (Philippians 2:5-11). Then he will change us, and we will no longer bear the image of the sinful man. We shall then bear the image of the heavenly one—namely Jesus! (1 Corinthians 15:49).

Declare to him his great and mighty deeds, and you will have touched upon the heart of worship!

Worship him for the sheer fact that he is the creator of all things. Come humbly to him as the clay would to the potter. Come in awe of his hands that fashioned even you. (I am in awe that the one who made all things would make me.)

> Come into his presence with thanksgiving; let us make a joyful noise to him with songs of praise! For *the* LORD *is a great God*, and *a great King above all gods*. In his hand are the depths of the earth; the heights of the mountains are his also. The sea is his, for he made it, and his hands formed the dry land. Oh come, let us *worship and bow down*; let

us *kneel before the* LORD, *our Maker*! For he is our God, and we are the people of his pasture, and the sheep of his hand.

Psalm 95: 1-7 (emphasis mine)

"The heavens declare the glory of God, and the sky above proclaims his handiwork" (Psalm 19:1). The heavens and the highest of heights praise him. Angels and all the angelic hosts of heaven exalt him. The sun, moon, and stars shine forth for his glory. The earth and all the creatures of the depths praise him with their voices lifted high. Hail, snow, mist, and stormy winds hasten to keep his Word! The mountains and their hills, the orchards, and the forests proclaim his worth. The wild and domesticated beasts declare his power along with the creeping things. The birds take flight to sing out the praises of the one who formed them. These all know who made them. These all boast in the powerful Creator and Sustainer of all things! So whether we are kings, princes, or servants, may we boast in our Maker. "Young men and maidens together, old men and children! Let them praise the name of the LORD, for his name alone is exalted; his majesty is above earth and heaven" (Psalm 148).

When you have recognized that you are the creature and that he is the Creator, you have started to take hold of what it is to worship.

If you find it difficult to worship him for his glory, strength, and holiness, it may be that you have not seen him clearly yet in the Scripture. If you find that you cannot recall his wonderful works and that to think on him as creator is less than satisfying, it may be that you have not come to love the revelation of him found in the Bible. Certainly, though, we should be able to worship him for our own salvation. His right hand and holy arm have worked salvation. He has declared to us his salvation and has revealed that he is righteous to all nations. He showed us steadfast love and faithfulness even when we showed him hatred and faithlessness. We should break forth into joyous singing! Let us dust off our guitars, polish our trumpets, and raise a joyful noise before all of heaven. Call the earth to join us and let the sea roar in the choir, for our Lord has saved and will judge the world in righteousness and all the people with equity (Psalm 98:1-9). The Bible has recorded for future generations how God looked down from his holy height; from heaven he looked at the earth. He turned his ear to the groans of the prisoners and set free those who were doomed to die because of sin. Let us praise him. Let us gather together all the kingdoms of the earth and let us worship the Lord (Psalm 102:18-22).

Only those who have tasted his salvation and have been clothed in his righteousness could worship him for his saving power. Only those who have been redeemed by the blood of Jesus, through the strong arm of our God, can break forth in joy at his judgment.

Christ bore our sorrows and grief. Jesus was stricken by God, wounded for our transgressions, and crushed for our iniquities—all that we might be called the children of God (Isaiah 53:4-5).

If we think upon the salvation that has been worked on our behalf when what we deserved was death, our hearts will explode in worship.

"Praise the LORD! For it is good to sing praises to our God; for it is pleasant, and a song of praise is fitting" Psalm 147:1. Yes, it is fitting that we should praise our God and that we should worship at his footstool. Let it be a pleasant thing to worship the Lord our Maker. Come to the word and know him deeply and intimately. The Bible will reveal to you the full character of this great and glorious God that we serve. Let worship become who we are at the very core as we understand our God better through the Holy Scriptures. May we fall upon our faces in the kitchen and declare his wonders. May we pull the car over to the side of the road and weep with joy over his goodness to us. May we raise our hands in praise as we lay in bed pouring over the Scripture. May we humbly lift a voice of exaltation to him from our prayer closets. Let us become worshipers! And when our knowledge of God has so flooded our hearts that worship could not be exhausted in a thousand millennia, let us join with others and lift up our worship as the Bride of Christ.

The hour "is now here, when the true worshipers will worship the Father in spirit and truth, for the Father is seeking such people to worship him. God is spirit, and those who worship him must worship in spirit and truth" (John 4: 23-24).

the necessity of Scripture in the revelation of Christ

We insist that we know Jesus, and yet we do not know the Scriptures that bear witness to him (John 5:39).

We are a privileged people. We are free to worship Christ and are free to proclaim our allegiance to him. We are literate. We have the Bible within easy reach. Yet our view of Christ has been more formed by popular culture than by the Word. The Jesus of the Bible has been traded for a cheap caricature that is weak and dispassionate. Jesus, who came to bring a sword instead of peace and division on the earth instead of unity, has been traded for an idol that finds all manner of worship acceptable (Matthew 10:34-39, Luke 12:49-53). Please note that the division Christ came to bring was not among the believers. For those who profess Christ, he desires unity. However, he is clear that the world will hate us on account of him, and that is where the division comes in.

A cultural Jesus who says, "If you do your best, you will be redeemed," has replaced the Jesus who came to proclaim that he was the only means by which we must be saved (John 14:6, John 3:16, John 3:36, Acts 4:12). The cultural Jesus, who is not bothered by sin, does not hold people to a standard of holiness, does not care if you are being conformed into his likeness, and teaches that there are ways to be saved apart from his work on the cross, is a lie! He is a fabrication of Biblically illiterate people who do not know the Jesus that they serve. We must come to the Scripture for we find the truth of the person of Jesus Christ therein.

It is not just the New Testament that speaks of Christ. As long as I live, I shall never forget a man I met doing ministry in 2000. He was in his late forties, and we began talking about the Bible. I mentioned something from the Old Testament, and he said, "Oh, I haven't read the Old Testament since they made me read it in seminary. The Old Testament doesn't really matter anymore anyway." I was floored! The Old Testament does not matter? The Old Testament speaks of Christ just as much as the New Testament. The Old Testament is replete with passages about our beautiful Savior!

When Jesus said that the Scriptures bore witness about him, he was talking about the Old Testament. After Jesus rose from the dead, he walked with two men along the road to Emmaus. They did not recognize him, and with deep sadness, they told him of the man named Jesus whom they thought was the Messiah who just days before had died. In bewilderment, they told of how that very morning the tomb he was laid in had been found empty.

Jesus listened to their story and then spoke to them.

> "How foolish you are, and how slow to believe all that the prophets have spoken! Did not the Messiah have to suffer these things and then enter his glory?" *And beginning with Moses and all the Prophets, he explained to them what was said in all the Scriptures concerning himself.*
>
> Luke 24:25-27 (emphasis mine)

Later, Jesus appeared to the eleven disciples and those who were gathered with them and said to them, "'This is what I told you while I was still with you: *Everything must be fulfilled that is written about me in the Law of Moses, the Prophets and the Psalms.'* Then he opened their minds so they could understand the Scriptures" (Luke 24: 44, 45).

Jesus's testimony is that the Law of Moses, the Prophets, and the Psalms all speak not only of who he is but also of what he would accomplish.

Consider what Peter said about the prophets who wrote about the salvation that we would inherit through Christ.

> Concerning this salvation, the prophets, who spoke of the grace that was to come to you, searched intently and with the greatest care, trying to find out the time and circumstances to which the Spirit

of Christ in them was pointing when he predicted the sufferings of the Messiah and the glories that would follow.

1 Peter 1:10-11

Even as the prophets spoke and wrote their messages from God, they knew that the things they taught were filled with truth about the coming of the Savior. They petitioned the Holy Spirit within them for understanding of the things they penned. Now their words have come alive for us because we know the beauty and horror of the cross and how our God died there for us. What they wrote can fully be appreciated only as it is understood and interpreted through the truth of Jesus.

David, a shepherd boy who became a king, was also a prophet. Certainly he wrote about things that were going on in his own life, but he also wrote about the coming and resurrection of our LORD. After Pentecost when the disciples had been filled with the Holy Spirit, Peter stood up to preach his first sermon.

> For David says concerning [Christ Jesus], "I saw the Lord always before me, for he is at my right hand that I may not be shaken; therefore my heart was glad, and my tongue rejoiced; my flesh also will dwell in hope. For you will not abandon my soul to Hades, or let your Holy One see corruption. You

have made known to me the paths of life; you will make me full of gladness with your presence."

Brothers, I may say to you with confidence about the patriarch David that he both died and was buried, and his tomb is with us to this day. *Being therefore a prophet*, and knowing that God had sworn with an oath to him that he would set one of his descendants on his throne, *[David] foresaw and spoke about the resurrection of the Christ*, that he was not abandoned to Hades, nor did his flesh see corruption. This Jesus God raised up, and of that we all are witnesses. Being therefore exalted at the right hand of God, and having received from the Father the promise of the Holy Spirit, he has poured out this that you yourselves are seeing and hearing. For David did not ascend into the heavens, but he himself says, "The Lord said to my Lord, Sit at my right hand, until I make your enemies your footstool."

Acts 2:25-35

Peter plainly stated here that David was not writing about himself in these passages from Psalm 16 and 110. Instead, David was writing these through the power of the Holy Spirit and was prophesying about the truth of the coming Messiah (Matthew 22:43, Mark 12:36). David had even written of Jesus's betrayal at the hands of Judas by the power of the Holy Spirit (Acts 1:15-20, Psalm 69:25, Psalm 109:8).

When reading the Old Testament, we can know that "no prophecy was ever produced by the will of man, but men spoke from God as they were carried along by the Holy Spirit" (2 Peter 1:21).

The Scripture in its entirety speaks to us of the wonderful truth of Jesus. We must, therefore, be dedicated students of the Word of God that we might intimately know the one who purchased us through his blood.

Consider how Psalm 22 portrays intimate details of the cross. As you read the section of this Psalm please note that I have included the New Testament references that fulfill the Davidic prophecies. Most of the prophecies will be recognizable to you. It becomes clear that David wasn't only writing about himself in Psalm 22 but was also writing about what would happen to Jesus the Messiah. See what Paul says concerning David in Acts 1:16, 2:30.

> My God, my God, why have you forsaken me…? (Matthew 27: 46) But I am a worm and not a man, scorned by mankind and despised by the people. All who see me mock me; they make mouths at me; they wag their heads (Matthew 27: 39, 41, 44, Luke 23:36). He trusts in the LORD; let him deliver him; let him rescue him, for he delights in him! (Matthew 27:43). Yet you are he who took me from the womb; you made me trust you at my mother's breasts. On you was I cast from my birth, and from my mother's womb you have been my God…I am poured out like water, and all my bones are out of

joint; my heart is like wax; it is melted within my breast; (John 19:34) my strength is dried up like a potsherd, and my tongue sticks to my jaws; (John 19:28, 29) you lay me in the dust of death. For dogs encompass me; a company of evildoers encircles me; they have pierced my hands and feet—I can count all my bones—they stare and gloat over me; they divide my garments among them, (John 19:23-24, 32, 36) and for my clothing they cast lots.

Psalm 22:1, 6-10, 14-18

The Old Testament does not speak only of the cross. It speaks over and over again of Jesus. Look at how many times the Gospels deliberately declare that the things surrounding the life of Jesus were to fulfill scripture. The section below contains a New Testament passage and a reference to the Old Testament text that was thus fulfilled. (Every emphasis mine).

"She will bear a son, and you shall call his name Jesus, for he will save his people from their sins." *All this took place to fulfill what the Lord had spoken by the prophet*: "Behold, the virgin shall conceive and bear a son, and they shall call his name Immanuel."

Matthew 1:21-23 (Isaiah 7:14).

And he rose and took the child and his mother by night and departed to Egypt and remained there until the death of Herod. *This was to fulfill what the Lord had spoken by the prophet*, "Out of Egypt I called my son."

Matthew 2:14-15 (Hosea 11:1).

Then Herod, when he saw that he had been tricked by the wise men, became furious, and he sent and killed all the male children in Bethlehem and in all that region who were two years old or under, according to the time that he had ascertained from the wise men. *Then was fulfilled what was spoken by the prophet Jeremiah*: "A voice was heard in Ramah, weeping and loud lamentation, Rachel weeping for her children; she refused to be comforted, because they are no more."

Matthew 2:16-18 (Jeremiah 31:15)

But when he heard that Archelaus was reigning over Judea in place of his father Herod, he was afraid to go there, and being warned in a dream he withdrew to the district of Galilee. And he went and lived in a city called Nazareth, *that what was spoken by the prophets might be fulfilled*: "He shall be called a Nazarene."

Matthew 2:22, 23

———————

And leaving Nazareth he went and lived in Capernaum by the sea, in the territory of Zebulun and Naphtali, so *that what was spoken by the prophet Isaiah might be fulfilled*: "The land of Zebulun and the land of Naphtali, the way of the sea, beyond the Jordan, Galilee of the Gentiles."

Matthew 4:13-17 (Isaiah 9:1-2)

———————

That evening they brought to him many who were oppressed by demons, and he cast out the spirits with a word and healed all who were sick. *This was to fulfill what was spoken by the prophet Isaiah*: "He took our illnesses and bore our diseases."

Matthew 8:16, 17 (Isaiah 53:4, 5)

———————

Jesus, aware of this, withdrew from there. And many followed him, and he healed them all and ordered them not to make him known. *This was to fulfill what was spoken by the prophet Isaiah*: "Behold, my servant whom I have chosen, my beloved with whom my soul is well pleased. I will put my Spirit upon him, and he will proclaim justice to the Gentiles. He will not quarrel or cry aloud, nor will anyone hear his voice in the streets; a bruised reed he will not break, and a smoldering wick he will not quench, until he brings justice to victory; and in his name the Gentiles will hope."

Matthew 12:15-21 (Isaiah 42:1-3)

———————

This is why I speak to them in parables, because seeing they do not see, and hearing they do not hear, nor do they understand. Indeed, in their case *the prophecy of Isaiah is fulfilled* that says: "'You will indeed hear but never understand, and you will indeed see but never perceive. For this people's heart has grown dull, and with their ears they can barely hear, and their eyes they have closed, lest they should see with their eyes and hear with their ears and understand with their heart and turn, and I would heal them.'"

Matthew 13:13-15 (Isaiah 6:9, 10).

———————

"If anyone says anything to you, you shall say, 'The Lord needs them,' and he will send them at once." *This took place to fulfill what was spoken by the prophet*, saying, "Say to the daughter of Zion, 'Behold, your king is coming to you, humble, and mounted on a donkey, and on a colt, the foal of a beast of burden.'"

Matthew 21:3-5 (Isaiah 62:11, Zechariah 9:9)

"Do you think that I cannot appeal to my Father, and he will at once send me more than twelve legions of angels? *But how then should the Scriptures be fulfilled, that it must be so?*" At that hour Jesus said to the crowds, "Have you come out as against a robber, with swords and clubs to capture me? Day after day I sat in the temple teaching, and you did not seize me. But all this has taken place that the Scriptures of the prophets might be fulfilled." Then all the disciples left him and fled.

Matthew 26:53-56 (Zechariah 13:7)

And he came to Nazareth, where he had been brought up. And as was his custom, he went to the synagogue on the Sabbath day, and he stood up to read. And the scroll of the prophet Isaiah was given to him. He unrolled the scroll and found the place where it was written, "The Spirit of the Lord is upon me, because he has anointed me to proclaim good news to the poor. He has sent me to proclaim liberty to the captives and recovering of sight to the blind, to set at liberty those who are oppressed, to proclaim the year of the Lord's favor." And he rolled up the scroll and gave it back to the attendant and sat down. And the eyes of all in the synagogue were fixed on him. And he began to say to them, *"Today this Scripture has been fulfilled in your hearing."*

Luke 4:16-21 (Isaiah 61:1-3)

For I tell you that *this Scripture must be fulfilled in me*: 'And he was numbered with the transgressors.' For what is written about me has its fulfillment.

Luke 22:37 (Isaiah 53:9, 12)

Though he had done so many signs before them, they still did not believe in him, *so that the word spoken by the prophet Isaiah might be fulfilled*: "Lord, who has believed what he heard from us, and to whom has the arm of the Lord been revealed?"

John 12:37, 38 (Isaiah 53:1)

If you know these things, blessed are you if you do them. I am not speaking of all of you; I know whom I have chosen. *But the Scripture will be fulfilled*, 'He who ate my bread has lifted his heel against me.' I am telling you this now, before it takes place, that when it does take place you may believe that I am he.

John 13:17-19 (Psalm 41:9)

But *the word that is written in their Law must be fulfilled*: "They hated me without a cause."

John 15:25 (Psalm 35:19)

While I was with them, I kept them in your name, which you have given me. I have guarded them, and not one of them has been lost except the son of destruction, *that the Scripture might be fulfilled*.

John 17:12 (Psalm 109:6-15)

But *what God foretold by the mouth of all the prophets*, that his Christ would suffer, *he thus fulfilled*.

Acts 3:18

> For those who live in Jerusalem and their rulers, because they did not recognize him nor understand *the utterances of the prophets*, which are read every Sabbath, *fulfilled them by condemning him.*

Acts 13:27

These are just a few of the places where the Old and New Testaments collide with great force. The beauty of our God, our Savior and our Teacher, can be found in the Scripture. In the pages of the Bible is where we come to have the true person of Jesus revealed to us. No longer settle for a cultural Jesus who changes with the times; rather, embrace the Jesus of Heaven! If we are not spending time in the Word, then we do not yet know him as we ought to. (To learn more about how the Old Testament foreshadows Christ, look for my book *The Shadow*.)

the necessity
of Scripture
in preaching

I recognize that there are few pastors reading this book. Most of you are just trying to learn even more of what it means to honor the Lord with your life. I am addressing this chapter to those who endeavor to preach the Word of God and have been especially gifted by God to proclaim it, but I want everyone to be challenged and encouraged through it, as well. Keep in mind that, even if you are not called by God to preach, we believers are all called to be salt and light in this dark world. Therefore it is imperative that what we say about the things of God be grounded in the truth of Scripture.

Sit under Biblical preachers. Be taught by men who hold tightly to the Word and loosely to worldly recognition. Cling to those who preach with all boldness—those who with zeal proclaim the full truth of Scripture. Weigh the preacher's words against the text and see that he is making Jesus known. If he is not preaching truth, find a new pastor!

If you are a pastor reading these words or one who is charged with the heavy responsibility of making known the truth of Jesus, I pray that this would challenge and encourage you, as well. We must be men who know nothing except Jesus Christ and him crucified (1 Corinthians 2:2). We are not to be concerned with lofty speech or wisdom. Our sole duty is the proclamation of the testimony of God (1 Corinthians 2:1). We preach the simple message of the gospel, not seeking to rob the cross of its power through words of eloquent wisdom (1 Corinthians 1:17). We preach the unsearchable riches of Christ crucified, dead, and resurrected (1 Corinthians 1:23, Ephesians 3:8). But somewhere along the way, the professional preacher became discontent with the name of Jesus and more concerned with making something of his own name.

The damning power of sin, the offense of the cross, and the redeeming work of Jesus's blood has been replaced in our pulpits with "sermons" on day planners and housework. So-called Bible studies are cropping up that focus on pottery and photography and are void of any mention of Christ Jesus. Sermons flood our churches on how to have a better self-image or how to line your pockets with cash, but few sermons are preached on the worth of following Christ or the riches of making him known. Many pastors are as Biblically starved as the sheep they shepherd. More time is spent researching an apt illustration than is spent on bended knee in prayerful examination of the text. Churches are growing more concerned with the weekly budget and attendance than they are with rightly proclaiming the word of truth. Other "churches" are being formed with no Bible teaching, no mention of Christ, no leadership, no baptism, no church discipline, no training in gifts, no standard for elders, and no expectation of holy living. We have exchanged the truth of God for a lie. We have exchanged the glory of our immortal God for images resembling mortal man (Romans 1:22-25). Job security and retirement have become of greater concern to us than obedience to our Maker.

This should not be so!

Paul says of Timothy, the pastor, that he has been acquainted with the Scripture from childhood. He then reminds Timothy that "All scripture is breathed out by God" and that it is useful for "teaching, reproof, correction, and for training in righteousness." The next thing that Paul says to him is this:

> "I charge you in the presence of God and of Christ Jesus, who is to judge the living and the dead, and by his appearing and his kingdom: *preach the Word*; be ready in season and out of season; reprove, rebuke, and exhort, with complete patience and teaching" (2 Timothy 3:14-4:2–emphasis mine).

"Timothy, the Word that you have been made familiar with since you were a child is good for training in righteousness, so *preach the Word*!" Be acquainted with the Word and then preach the Word!

Now the truth is that most of us as preachers were not trained in the Scripture from our childhood. My parents were diligent to take me to church. They taught me to pray and to tithe. I was taught early about God, but I was far from being truly acquainted with the Bible. Still, that is no excuse to remain uninformed. Once we have become acquainted with the Word, we immediately recognize its value in making us competent followers of Christ. Yet too often our messages are free from the power of it.

This can only be one of two things. Either we do not really know the Word to begin with, or we do not revere it as we should.

I am constantly challenged by the truth of Matthew 12:34. "You brood of vipers! How can you speak good when you are evil? For *out of the abundance of the heart, the mouth speaks*" (emphasis mine). Perhaps the reason the words of Christ do not pour forth from our mouths is because we have not yet hidden them in our hearts. A good test to judge where our hearts are is to listen to what our mouths are saying. We cannot help but speak of that which is hidden in the chambers of our heart.

This is a truth for all believers. We must all be so filled with the Word of God that we cannot help but proclaim it. However, most Christians are so scripturally destitute that they find it easier to talk about the football game, the reality show, and the weather than they do the life-giving words of God. It is not only the preacher whose heart must be filled with Scripture.

As preachers, many of us fill our sermons with more illustrations, jokes, and rhetoric than we do Scripture because those things have taken up greater room in our hearts. Yet we are to keep God's Word within our hearts, and then we are to guard our hearts with great care, for from them flow the springs of life (Proverbs 4:20-23). Our hearts are to be storehouses of truth. If the Word of God is really in our hearts, it will be impossible for us to contain it. Like a fire shut up in our bones, we will blaze from the inside out until we are weary of holding it in. Then, like a volcano, it will erupt from our lips (Jeremiah 20:9). If we know the glad news of deliverance, our lips cannot be restrained. The message of salvation cannot be hidden in our hearts—kept there under lock and key. We who love the message of the cross are compelled to preach the stead-fast love and faithfulness of God to the great congregation. We are pressed to proclaim his wondrous deeds (Psalm 40: 4-10).

When our tongues have fallen silent and we find that no pulpit has been opened to us, necessity is laid upon us like a mountain, and we cry out, "Woe is me if I do not preach the gospel!" (1 Corinthians 9:15-18). When we have stood in the counsel of God, we will proclaim his words to his people. We will not preach our own dreams or the inventions of our own hearts. We who have the Word of God will speak that word faithfully. For our dreams and inventions have no more in common with biblical truth than straw has in common with wheat (Jeremiah 23:21-28). When we come to the place where we believe that our thoughts and reasoning have greater value than the words of God and that our traditions and customs are more practical than the beautiful law of God, we have become guilty of the Pharisees' sin (Matthew 15:1-9).

We have forgotten that the Bible is not mere words but the very source of life to us (Deuteronomy 32:47). We have failed to remember that our words are vain, but the words of God are like rain and snow from heaven that accomplish the purpose for which they were sent (Isaiah 55:10-11). We have neglected the Word because we know that it is a fire that will ignite our lives, and it is a hammer that will break our stony hearts into pieces (Jeremiah 23:29). We would rather not (or we believe our sheep would rather not) be pierced to the division of soul and spirit to joints and marrow, discerning the thoughts and intentions of the heart (Hebrews 4:12). We would rather have the crowd leave with smiles on their faces than changes in their hearts. We have found the Scripture too invasive and too surgical. If that is where we stand, we have become pitiful, indeed.

There are throngs of people who will not endure sound teaching, and sadly there are heaps of teachers ready to accommodate their itching ears (2 Timothy 4:3, 4). But we will not preach for them. Others will demand that we stop preaching in the name of Christ, but we will press on, knowing that it is right in the sight of God to obey him rather than men. We cannot stop speaking about what we have seen and heard in the word (Acts 4:17-19). We will preach for the glory of our God and the exaltation of our Lord. We will not preach words taught in human wisdom, but we will teach words full of the Holy Spirit and power (1 Corinthians 2:4). We will set our hearts to study the Law of the Lord to practice it and to teach it to those in our charge (Ezra 7:10). We will eat the words of God like honey, and they will become the delight of our hearts (Psalm 19:10, Jeremiah 15:16). We will remember that those of us who have the ambition to teach will incur a stricter judgment by God, and we will tremble under the weight of his word (James 3:1). We will read from the book, from the Law of God, and we will clearly give the sense of it so that our hearers can understand (Nehemiah 8:8). We will show ourselves to be proven workers of God handling the Word of God accurately, cutting a straight road of truth without even a hint of deviation (2 Timothy 2:15).

We will not forget that every day souls are being taken away to death and people are stumbling to the slaughter. We will show mercy to them and snatch them out of the fire. We must not say, "We did not know this," because God weighs our hearts and perceives this (Proverbs 24:11-12, Jude 22, 23). He has appointed us for the task of proclaiming salvation.

> Everyone who calls on the name of the Lord will be saved. But how are they to call on him in whom they have not believed? And how are they to believe in him of whom they have never heard? And how are they to hear without someone preaching? And how are they to preach unless they are sent? As it is written, "How beautiful are the feet of those who preach the good news!" *So faith comes from hearing and hearing through the word of Christ.*
>
> Romans 10:13-17 (emphasis mine)

The comic can focus on making his hearers laugh, but let the preacher proclaim Christ! The politician can be concerned with earning points and favor, but let the preacher proclaim Christ! The motivational speaker can seek to make people feel better about themselves, but let the preacher proclaim Christ!

final admonition

Here we are at a junction. The time has come again (or perhaps this is the first time) for us to decide to be people of the Word. We must decide in this moment to love it and to hoard it in our hearts. It will set us free from sin and give us power for holy living. The Word of God will train our eyes for the return of Christ.

The Word will come alive in our families. Husband, wife, and children will be changed because of it. Husbands will become more like Jesus in the love of their brides. Wives will learn to be gracious and find their families strong and won to Christ. Children will find their lives blessed as they learn to obey their parents, not for the parents' sake but for the purpose of honoring God.

Worship will rise up in our souls like a whelming flood. We will declare in worship God's strength, glory, holiness, salvation, love, power, mercy, righteousness, and judgment. We will be compelled by his goodness such that our mouths will never be shut. Praise and worship will live in our hearts and daily pour from our lips. When we worship this way we will see that those around us will worship our beautiful God as well.

We will know Jesus more deeply than we ever have before, adoring him in the Old Testament. The prophecies of Isaiah will turn our minds to Jesus. David's Psalms will reveal to us the truth of Christ's crucifixion. Genesis will paint for us the picture of redemption. We will find that the Old and New Testaments are not divided but are in perfect unity.

We will preach the unadulterated message of Jesus (or hear preachers who do). We will realize that the time is too short to give our audience anything less than Jesus. Fiery, graceful, beautiful truth will fall from our pulpits like rain and we will be unashamed of the gospel we preach. Like Paul, we will boast in nothing but the cross. Like Jeremiah, we will find the word to be a fire in our bones. Though we may be tempted to hold it in we will find that we can't. And for all of our biblical teaching we will find that our hearers are truly changed into the image of Christ and equipped to honor him.

A year from now, we will look back on who we were, and we will see that we have begun to mature. Day upon day, we will be regaled with even more of the riches of God and the feasts of his table. In the following pages, you will find a Bible reading plan to help you get started and a few hints and tips on how to read.

Press deeply into the word that you may press deeply into the heart of God.

I am excited for you, because I know that you will never be the same.

hints and tips
for reading

I have a rule when I read the Bible; I must believe everything it says, and I must stop where it is silent. I typically say it this way: "I'll go as far as the Bible goes, and I'll quit where it quits." What I mean by that is that I will not be shaped by Christian clichés or what grandma used to say. Nor will I be shaped by verses out of context or, for that matter, verses that do not exist. "God helps those who help themselves" is not a Bible verse; it is not even good theology. "Cleanliness is next to godliness" cannot be found in the Scripture. "When God closes a door, he opens a window" is a nice thought, but not only is it not biblical, it is not true. There were many people who followed God in faithful obedience who lost everything, including their lives. Doors were shut for them, and then they died. But they were right where they should have been in the middle of God's sovereign will. When we begin to read the Scripture, we will weed these worthless clichés out of our lives.

More important is the fact that when we stay biblically illiterate, we use the Bible itself out of context. This is a dangerous thing to do. When we are reading, we do not get to just lift a single verse off the page. Instead, we must consider the chapter the verse is in. What is that chapter saying? We need to think on the book the verse is in. What is the book about? Who is the book written to? We need to look at that verse in light of the rest of the Bible to see if it is in line with the rest of what God says. We do not go to the Bible to prove a point or win an argument or get bullets for our spiritual guns. We read the Bible to be changed. Let us look at a few examples.

"Look among the nations, and see; wonder and be astounded. For I am doing a work in your days that you would not believe if told" (Habakkuk 1:5). I have heard this verse used so many times in a positive light. I have seen it on camp shirts. It has been the theme for retreats and revivals. I even saw it as the advertising point for a conference that packed a stadium with twenty-five thousand people. People always say, "This is such an encouraging verse. I just know that God is going to do a work at this event that we won't even believe." Every time I see this verse used this way, I cringe. If you read Habakkuk 1, you will find that the "work" God is about to do is to utterly destroy those who have rebelled against him. This book is a prophecy against the rebellious people of Israel who have turned to other gods. Even when this verse is quoted in Acts 13:41, Paul tells the audience to "believe" in Christ but that those who do not should "beware" lest the word of Habakkuk come upon them (Acts 13:35-41). He tells them to "beware!" This is not a verse of encouragement. It is a verse of warning! We do not get to use the Bible however we want to.

How about this next verse? "Seek first the kingdom of God and his righteousness and all these things will be added to you" (Matthew 6:33). This verse gets used for everything. People claim this verse for cars, jobs, raises, houses, vacations, boats, kids, and any number of other things. But if you begin reading in verse 25, you will see that the passage is concerned with what you will eat and what you will wear. In verse 31, we are told not to be anxious about food or clothing. In verse 32, we are told that God knows we need these things. *Then* comes famous verse 33. Now we understand that "all these things" refers to food and clothing. Paul, at the end of his life, wrote to Timothy. "But if we have food and clothing, with these we will be content" (1 Timothy 6:8). Jacob in Genesis 28:20 is concerned with food and clothing. Even in Deuteronomy at the end of the forty years in the wilderness, God makes it clear that he took care of the need for food and clothing in that time (Deuteronomy 8:1-4). God's promise in Matthew 6:33 is concerned with food and clothing.

We take many verses out of context. Jeremiah 29:11 was written to a group of people who were taken into slavery. They had been gone for two years and had sixty-eight more years to go. Most of the people reading that verse would die before it was fulfilled. It is about the restoration of the people to Jerusalem. Yet we use it for our own personal situations. Another example is Philippians 4:13, which is talking about all the circumstances of life that have come upon Paul during his service of God. He is saying that whether he has plenty or lack and whether he is hungry or well fed, he is able to handle all circumstances through Christ who gives him strength. This verse does not apply to taking a test or bowling a perfect game or running a marathon.

It is imperative that we understand the context of the Bible so that we can have our lives changed by it.

Do not just read small bits and pieces. It is hard to get the sense of something unless you are reading at least a few chapters at a time. As Bible reading becomes easier for you, try reading an entire book in one sitting.

Make notes for yourself either in a journal or right in the margin of your Bible.

Ask lots of questions. In fact, the moment we run out of questions, we can be certain that we are too full of pride. Questions are not bad or signs of weakness. Sometimes it is our questions that have us press back into the Bible. Have a pastor friend on speed dial who you can discuss scripture with. (I have about four.) Pick people who are older in the faith than you by ten or twenty years (or at least older in Bible study) and glean from them. Talk to them about what you are reading.

Memorize it! The more you memorize, the better you will understand it!

Buy some highlighters that you like. I know it sounds silly, but it will help you remember things if you highlight verses that God is using to speak to you.

Use the Bible plan below or find one online that you like. If you get bogged down in your reading feel free to skip around from section to section, but at some point read a book straight through.

Talk to other people. See how they read and follow their example.

The Bible plan below is a compilation of several different online plans. The order is designed for people who are new to Bible reading. You will find that every day of the week you are looking at something different. One day may be an Epistle, the next part of the Law. You will have history mixed with the wisdom books and then the next day will find you in the Gospels. I personally don't like to jump around this much, but you may find it helpful if you are brand new to Bible reading. If, however, you are well set in your Bible reading, please stick with the plan that works for you.

What is the correct way to read the Bible? Open it up and read!

Romans 1-2

Genesis 1-3

Joshua 1-5

Psalms 1-2

Job 1-2

Isaiah 1-6

Matthew 1-2

Romans 3-4

Genesis 4-7

Joshua 6-10

Psalms 3-5

Job 3-4

Isaiah 7-11

Matthew 3-4

Romans 5-6

Genesis 8-11

Joshua 11-15

Psalms 6-8

Job 5-6

Isaiah 12-17

Matthew 5-7

Romans 7-8

Genesis 12-15

Joshua 16-20

Psalms 9-11

Job 7-8

Isaiah 18-22

Matthew 8-10

Romans 9-10

Genesis 16-19

Joshua 21-24

Psalms 12-14

Job 9-10

Isaiah 23-28

Matthew 11-13

Romans 11-12

Genesis 20-23

Judges 1-6

Psalms 15-17

Job 11-12

Isaiah 29-33

Matthew 14-16

Romans 13-14

Genesis 24-27

Judges 7-11

Psalms 18-20

Job 13-14

Isaiah 34-39

Matthew 17-19

Romans 15-16

Genesis 28-31

Judges 12-16

Psalms 21-23

Job 15-16

Isaiah 40-44
Matthew 20-22
1 Corinthians 1-2
Genesis 32-35
Judges 17-21
Psalms 24-26
Job 17-18
Isaiah 45-50
Matthew 23-25
1 Corinthians 3-4
Genesis 36-39
Ruth
Psalms 27-29
Job 19-20
Isaiah 51-55
Matthew 26-28
1 Corinthians 5-6
Genesis 40-43
1 Sam 1-5
Psalms 30-32
Job 21-22
Isaiah 56-61
Mark 1-2
1 Corinthians 7-8
Genesis 44-47
1 Samuel 6-10
Psalms 33-35

Job 23-24
Isaiah 62-66
Mark 3-4
1 Corinthians 9-10
Genesis 48-50
1 Samuel 11-15
Psalms 36-38
Job 25-26
Jeremiah 1-6
Mark 5-6
1 Corinthians 11-12
Exodus 1-4
1 Samuel 16-20
Psalms 39-41
Job 27-28
Jeremiah 7-11
Mark 7-8
1 Corinthians 13-14
Exodus 5-8
1 Samuel 21-25
Psalms 42-44
Job 29-30
Jeremiah 12-16
Mark 9-10
1 Corinthians 15-16
Exodus 9-12
1 Samuel 26-31

Psalms 45-47
Job 31-32
Jeremiah 17-21
Mark 11-12
2 Corinthians 1-3
Exodus 13-16
2 Samuel 1-4
Psalms 48-50
Job 33-34
Jeremiah 22-26
Mark 13-14
2 Corinthians 4-5
Exodus 17-20
2 Samuel 5-9
Psalms 51-53
Job 35-36
Jeremiah 27-31
Mark 15-16
2 Corinthians 6-8
Exodus 21-24
2 Samuel 10-14
Psalms 54-56
Job 37-38
Jeremiah 32-36
Luke 1-2
2 Corinthians 9-10
Exodus 25-28

2 Samuel 15-19
Psalms 57-59
Job 39-40
Jeremiah 37-41
Luke 3-4
2 Corinthians 11-13
Exodus 29-32
2 Samuel 20-24
Psalms 60-62
Job 41-42
Jeremiah 42-46
Luke 5-6
Galatians 1-3
Exodus 33-36
1 Kings 1-4
Psalms 63-65
Proverbs 1
Jeremiah 47-52
Luke 7-8
Galatians 4-6
Exodus 37-40
1 Kings 5-9
Psalms 66-68
Proverbs 2-3
Lamentations
Luke 9-10
Ephesians 1-3

Leviticus 1-3
1 Kings 10-13
Psalms 69-71
Proverbs 4
Ezekiel 1-6
Luke 11-12
Ephesians 4-6
Leviticus 4-6
1 Kings 14-18
Psalms 72-74
Proverbs 5-6
Ezekiel 7-12
Luke 13-14
Philippians 1-2
Leviticus 7-9
1 Kings 19-22
Psalms 75-77
Proverbs 7
Ezekiel 13-18
Luke 15-16
Philippians 3-4
Leviticus 10-12
2 Kings 1-5
Psalms 78-80
Proverbs 8-9
Ezekiel 19-24
Luke 17-18

Colossians 1-2
Leviticus 13-15
2 Kings 6-10
Psalms 81-83
Proverbs 10
Ezekiel 25-30
Luke 19-20
Colossians 3-4
Leviticus 16-18
2 Kings 11-15
Psalms 84-86
Proverbs 11-12
Ezekiel 31-36
Luke 21-22
1 Thessalonians 1-3
Leviticus 19-21
2 Kings 16-20
Psalms 87-89
Proverbs 13
Ezekiel 37-42
Luke 23-24
1 Thessalonians 4-5
Leviticus 22-24
2 Kings 21-25
Psalms 90-92
Proverbs 14-15
Ezekiel 43-48

John 1-2
2 Thessalonians
Leviticus 25-27
1 Chronicles 1-4
Psalms 93-95
Proverbs 16
Daniel 1-6
John 3-4
1 Timothy 1-3
Numbers 1-4
1 Chronicles 5-9
Psalms 96-98
Proverbs 17-18
Daniel 7-12
John 5-6
1 Timothy 4-6
Numbers 5-8
1 Chronicles 10-14
Psalms 99-101
Proverbs 19
Hosea 1-7
John 7-9
2 Timothy 1-2
Numbers 9-12
1 Chronicles 15-19
Psalms 102-104
Proverbs 20-21

Hosea 8-14
John 10-12
2 Timothy 3-4
Numbers 13-16
1 Chronicles 20-24
Psalms 105-107
Proverbs 22
Joel
John 13-15
Titus
Numbers 17-20
1 Chronicles 25-29
Psalms 108-110
Proverbs 23-24
Amos 1-4
John 16-18
Philemon
Numbers 21-24
2 Chronicles 1-5
Psalms 111-113
Proverbs 25
Amos 5-9
John 19-21
Heb 1-4
Numbers 25-28
2 Chronicles 6-10
Psalms 114-116

Proverbs 26-27
Obadiah
Acts 1-2
Heb 5-7
Numbers 29-32
2 Chronicles 11-15
Psalms 117-118
Proverbs 28
Jonah
Acts 3-4
Hebrews 8-10
Numbers 33-36
2 Chronicles 16-20
Psalms 119
Proverbs 29-30
Micah
Acts 5-6
Hebrews 11-13
Deuteronomy 1-3
2 Chronicles 21-24
Psalms 120-121
Proverbs 31
Nahum
Acts 7-8
James 1-3
Deuteronomy 4-6
2 Chronicles 25-28

Psalms 122-124
Ecclesiastes 1-2
Habakkuk
Acts 9-10
James 4-5
Deuteronomy 7-9
2 Chronicles 29-32
Psalms 125-127
Ecclesiastes 3-4
Zephaniah
Acts 11-12
1 Peter 1-3
Deuteronomy 10-12
2 Chronicles 33-36
Psalms 128-130
Ecclesiastes 5-6
Haggai
Acts 13-14
1 Peter 4-5
Deuteronomy 13-15
Ezra 1-5
Psalms 131-133
Ecclesiastes 7-8
Zechariah 1-7
Acts 15-16
2 Peter
Deuteronomy 16-19

Ezra 6-10
Psalms 134-136
Ecclesiastes 9-10
Zechariah 8-14
Acts 17-18
1 John 1-3
Deuteronomy 20-22
Nehemiah 1-4
Psalms 137-139
Ecclesiastes 11-12
Malachi
Acts 19-20
1 John 4-5
Deuteronomy 23-25
Nehemiah 5-9
Psalms 140-142
Song of Solomon 1-2
Revelation 1-6
Acts 21-22
2 John
Deuteronomy 26-28
Nehemiah 10-13
Psalms 143-145
Song of Solomon 3-4
Revelation 7-11
Acts 23-24
3 John

Deuteronomy 29-31
Esther 1-5
Psalms 146-148
Song of Solomon 5-6
Revelation 12-17
Acts 25-26
Jude
Deuteronomy 32-34
Esther 6-10
Psalms 149-150
Song of Solomon 7-8
Revelation 18-22
Acts 27-28